LEE HYEONSE

이현세

Daniel Choy ǀ Yun Hyeji

 영진미디어

LEE HYEONSE

Daniel Choy | Yun Hyeji

OZEKO 영진미디어

이 책의 난이도

이 책은 '영어로 읽는 세계 속 한국인' 시리즈입니다. 초등학교 고학년에서 중학생까지 읽기에 적당한 수준이며, 뒤쪽으로 갈수록 어휘가 다양해집니다. 12세~15세 청소년 대상의 TOEFL Junior를 준비하고 있는 학생들이 보기에 적절합니다.

초등학교 고학년			중학생		
11세	12세	13세	14세	15세	16세

기준	난이도
단어	2000 단어 내외
문법	시제를 구분하고 구와 절의 문장 구조를 이해할 수 있는 정도
독해	글을 읽고 정확한 내용을 파악하여, 질문에 답하거나 다음 내용을 추론할 수 있는 종합적인 사고력을 지닌 정도

※ 청담 어학원의 Tera, Bridge, Par 레벨, 토피아 어학원의 HT4, GB, G1 레벨, 아발론 어학원의 JB, JI, JA 레벨 정도의 학생들이 보기에 적절합니다.

PREFACE

'The series of Korean in the world to read in English'
is a series of stories about famous Koreans from various
walks of life presenting their lives and achievements in
English. This book is an easy and fun read for young
people, its major class of readers, and a great way both
to learn English and to find out more about today's
heroes and what makes them so great.

Each chapter consists of beautifully illustrated pages.
As the book is composed only in English, the reader

is able to read and understand the English language at his or her own pace, mastering vocabulary, sentence structure and reading skills. The accompanied FILE recording of the text will improve listening skills while the downloadable PDF version of the Korean text will help with reading comprehension. The text is available at the YoungJinMedia website at www.yjbooks.co.kr and the FILE recording of the text is available at the YoungJinMedia IBlug at yjmedia.iblug.com.

The fifth story of our series features comic book artist Lee Hyeonse. With works like 『The Baseball Team』, Hyeonse helped Korea's comic book industry usher in a golden era. Let's listen to how this strong, passionate and optimistic artist grew up to become the iconic artist he is today.

CONTENTS

Lee Hyeonse is a comic book artist
through and through, now and forever.

1. Comic Book is My Life

"Hyeonse! Where are you? You really did it this time. Just wait till I catch you!"

His grandmother's angry voice shook up the neighborhood. Even some old men playing chess were **jolted** by her fury. Stray dogs would hide and cower at her **thunderous** shouting. But the young Lee Hyeonse was consumed in his comic book,

■ **jolt** [dʒoult] ⓝ.ⓥ move or cause to move with a sudden jerky motion
■ **thunderous** [θʌndərəs] ⓐ loud enough to cause temporary hearing loss

laughing away. He could shut out the noise around him when reading comic books. The fictional and non-fictional comic book characters came to life in the eyes of the young boy. While **immersed**▪ in his world of comic books, Hyeonse could be anyone, ranging from generals to superheroes. Suddenly he was pulled back into reality as his grandmother grabbed him by the collar.

"Comic books again!?"
"Grandma! No!"

She dragged him to a toilet. She would force his head into the dirty toilet bowl. He would

▪ **immerse** [imə́ːrs] ⓥ devote fully to

struggle to get free, but she was too strong for the little boy. The **stench** was unbearable.

"Didn't I warn you about what I'd do to you if you read comic books?"

"I'm sorry, I swear I won't read comic books. Never again!"

"You swear? You better keep that promise."

She gradually let go of him. After getting some fresh air, he could finally breathe. Back in those days, comic books were perceived to be not very educational and even harmful to children. It's no surprise that Hyeonse's grandmother didn't approve

■ **stench** [stentʃ] ⓝ a distinctive odor that is offensively unpleasant

of him reading such things. However, his promise was short lived. He would return to the comic book store, and she would drag him out of there again. It was only natural for him, as he was simply crazy about comic books.

Hyeonse chanced upon comic books and instantly fell in love with all they have to offer. Because his family was too poor to afford television or radio sets, comic books were the only way for him to gain access to different lives, stories and worlds of imagination.

Hyeonse was a very curious and **observant**▪ child. He had a knack for drawing something he saw, and he did it well. He wasn't satisfied just

▪ **observant** [əbzə́ːrvənt] ⓐ paying close attention especially to details

reading comic books. He would draw anything using any materials, be it pen and paper or stick and sand. All day long, he would draw until there was no more space in his notebooks and in the school field. Sometimes, he would be so focused on drawing, he'd skip meals and carry on through the night. Even with sticks he could bring to life everything from his imagination.

It took one small event in his life to help him make up his mind to become a comic book artist. One day, his friend Han Daehee who moved to Seoul, sent him some Japanese and American comic books. Hyeonse was simply blown away. Compared to Korean comic books, the Japanese and American ones were appealing in a different level. Hyeonse could not easily get over the fact that comic book cultures in these countries were far more developed.

'I can't believe these are comic books! They're more like works of art.'

This was the beginning of the legacy of Lee Hyeonse, one of the greatest Korean comic book artists.

2. Family Tragedy

Born in 1954 in Heunghae, North Gyeongsang Province, Lee Hyeonse grew up in Gyeongju, a place rich in Korean history. Being the only son, he was the most loved and **treasured** family member. If he napped, everyone kept quiet and gave him space. It is thanks to this background that he grew up to be confident and possess an **indomitable** spirit.

But he did experience some turbulence growing

▪ **treasure** [tréʒər] ⓝ,ⓥ hold dear

▪ **indomitable** [indάmətəbl] ⓐ impossible to subdue

up. His grandmother lost her husband at a young age, and had to do many odd jobs to provide for her three sons. His second uncle left for China to look for better jobs, and help the family out. Tragically, the Korean War broke out and his uncle was unable to return to South Korea. He ended up serving as an officer for the North Korean army. Because of this family relation, Hyeonse's father was dragged in for **interrogation**▪ by the South Korean military. That was the last they saw of him. The youngest of the three brothers was electrocuted to death in an accident at work in Gyeongju Station. After losing all of her children, she dedicated her life to taking care of the **widowed**▪

▪ **interrogation** [ìntèrəgéiʃən] ⓝ a sentence of inquiry that asks for a reply
▪ **widowed** [wídoud] ⓐ single because of death of the spouse

wives and their children.

One day, a letter arrived. It was from Hyeonse's second uncle who was forced to live in the North. Upon receiving it, his grandmother's eyes immediately began to shed tears. She took the letter to her room and called Hyeonse over.

"Read it for me, quick."

Whenever she received letters from the North, she would ask Hyeonse to read it for her. With each line **recited**", her eyes turned redder as she swallowed back the tears. After each reading, she would hold Hyeonse's hands and plead him this.

▪ **recite** [risáit] Ⓥ narrate or give a detailed account of

"Don't ever tell anyone about your uncle's letters from North Korea. We could get into trouble if someone finds out."

These were rare instances when he felt very uneasy. Sometime in the 1950s when the Korean War broke out on June 25th, before Hyeonse was born, the uncle serving in North Korean army dropped by his mother's home to give her a thick roll of North Korean **currency**▪. She treasured that roll of notes. She keeps it safe, waiting for that moment when she will be reunited with her son. No one in the family knew about it. But his sister took some of those notes with her to school for

▪ **currency** [kəˈrrənsi] ⓝ the metal or paper medium of exchange that is presently used

show and tell. Her teacher was shocked, and asked her where she got it from.

"Where did you find this? You can get into trouble because of it."

"I found it on the street."

"This is North Korean currency. If you get caught with it, you could get **arrested**▪. Next time, don't pick it up and just walk away."

She was scared senseless by her teacher's questions. Thankfully she lied her way out of the sticky situation. Upon hearing what happened, their grandmother immediately burned away all of

▪ **arrest** [ərést] ⓝ,ⓥ take into custody

the North Korean currency. She was heartbroken, after burning the prized memento of the son she lost. She cried and cried throughout the day. Hyeonse remembers that moment vividly, as one of the most painful and sad memories of his life.

3. Choosing the Path

Lee Hyeonse's family was so poor that they could barely afford barley porridge for meals. Not surprisingly he had little or no toys or games to play with. That's why he turned to affordable comic books. But back then, in Korea, comic books were perceived as harmful materials. Naturally his grandmother became worried. Hyeonse was often caught reading them in class and had them

confiscated▪. Thanks to his love for comic books, his drawing skills improved.

In middle school and high school, he was deeply involved in art club activities. He dreamed of becoming an artist someday, and getting into an art college was his immediate goal. But upon graduating high school, he learned that he was partially color blind. During those days, art college applicants with such conditions were not accepted. Not knowing what else he should do, he felt lost and sad. **Infuriated**▪ by this cruel twist of fate, he spent many days meaninglessly. It was a very trying period for young Hyeonse.

▪ **confiscate** [kánfəskèit] ⓐ,ⓥ take temporary possession of as a security, by legal authority

▪ **infuriate** [infjúərièit] ⓥ make furious

'Why can't I live for my dreams?'

But Hyeonse was an optimist, and he could soon shake off the doubts and disappointments. He decided to get back on his feet and fight for his dreams.

'Getting into art college isn't the only way. Perhaps this is a sign from a higher power, telling me to become a great comic book artist on my own. I'll do just that.'

And then, he had another idea.

'To become a good comic book artist, I need to be a good writer, so I should study writing.'

Back in those days, drawing skills were considered far more important than writing to become a good comic book artist. Hyeonse was clearly thinking outside the box with this idea. But this proved to be an important turning point in his journey. The literature and writing classes he attended back then helped him mature into a comic book artist that can write unique and well **plotted**▪ stories that touched readers. Hyeonse went back to Seoul to resume his studies. While preparing for his entrance exams, he sneaked into

▪ **plotted** [plated] ⓐ planned in advance

Seorabeol Art College lectures. Many respected novelists conducted special lectures there. He learned a lot about the principles of writing and literature there. Hyeonse was blessed to be able to learn from some of the best in the industry. Also, he worked under comic book artist Ha Yeongjo when not in class. Step by step, he was working towards his dreams.

In no time, summer arrived. During summer break, Hyeonse went back to Gyeongju, his hometown. He felt warm and welcomed there. But it was during this time, that another big incident that would change his life as an artist occurred. His relatives gathered at his home for the traditional ancestral rites. Everyone was somehow extra friendly to him.

"Remember me? I was a close friend of your father. I used to talk about you all the time."

After a while, he sensed something was amiss. His father described by the friend was quite different from the person he knew.

"Are you by any chance talking about my uncle?"
"Oh, you're right. My mistake. Sorry."

Hyeonse sensed something was not quite right. He could not help wonder if his relatives are hiding some secrets from him. So he went and asked a different relative.

"Remember how my dad died of electrocution?"

"Of course I do. He worked with him at Gyeongju station. So now you know that he is your real dad."

"What? My uncle was actually my father?"

Hyeonse felt like his world was **crumbling** down. He dashed to his grandmother and **confronted** her.

■ **crumble** [krʌmbl] ⓥ fall apart
■ **confront** [kənfrʌnt] ⓥ be face to face with

"Is it true what they said about my father? I'm not my father's son?"

"Hyeonse! You've finally learned the truth. Let me explain everything to you."

It was a shocking moment for Hyeonse. His grandmother held him tight and cried. Hyeonse couldn't hold back the tears either. They cried a river that day. Hyeonse had a hard time accepting the truth. His uncle was actually his real father and his sister was his cousin, and his two cousins were his real brothers. After her eldest son was killed by the Military police, Hyeonse's grandmother took Hyeonse in as that man's son, in order to keep the family **lineage**∎ alive. Upon learning this truth, Hyeonse could not face his real mother. It was extremely difficult for his family to finally reveal the truth after so many years of secrecy. Hyeonse had to disappear.

"I'm sorry. I just need to get away from you all. Maybe, after I can gather my thoughts, I'll see you again."

Hyeonse found a place to stay in Moraenae, Seoul, where most comic book artists were based. He chose to immerse himself in comic book making. After **pondering**∎ ways to debut as a

∎ **lineage** [láinidʒ] ⓝ the descendants of one individual

∎ **ponder** [pándər] ⓥ reflect deeply on a subject

comic book artist, he decided to ask any known artist to take him in as a pupil. He went to his friend Han Daehee, who was working as comic book artist in Seoul. Daehee is also the friend who first exposed Hyeonse to the world of foreign comic books. With a fist full of loose change, Hyeonse met up with his old friend.

"Daehee, long time no see. I came to Seoul to become a comic book artist. Help me out."

"I'm sure you'll make a fine artist someday, perhaps one of the best."

"That will be the day!"

"I kid you not! I remember the comic

strips you created when you were in 6th grade. Compared to what kids our age could create, yours had excellent storyline and great pace."

"You remember that! You must have a photographic memory."

The two friends made a list of all known comic book artists, and visited every one of them. But it wasn't easy to be accepted as a pupil. Hyeonse was very quiet, inexpressive and gave a cold first impression. Not many artists would be thrilled to take him in. Fortunately, Na Hana, who usually creates melodramatic comics accepted Hyeonse. Hyeonse moved into Hana's tiny home to learn the trade while working and living with the artist. Living with Hana was not exactly luxurious. The two could only afford 2 meals a day. And they could only have 1 rice meal a day. But despite the hardship, Hyeonse was thrilled to be pursuing his dreams. Under Hana's **tutelage**■, Hyeonse learned to write more emotional lines, and create more detailed background for his characters. But then he faced a big dilemma. Hyeonse had a style all his own. He yearned to create rough and tough characters. But while working for Hana, he would be painting more **feminine**■ and delicate objects like flowers and stars. In the end, Hyeonse left Hana and joined

■**tutelage** [tjúːtəlidʒ] ⑩ teaching pupils individually

■**feminine** [fémənin] ⓐ,⑩ befitting or characteristic of a woman

Lee Jeongmin's team which created comic books closer to Hyeonse's style of choice.

4. Learning from Different Studios

It was tough working under Lee Jeongmin. Hyeonse had to wake up at 5am everyday. First order of the day was setting the newspapers for the others to read. Ink as we know it today wasn't readily available back in those days, so he had to grind old-fashioned stick ink for the others to use. It was a demanding process, and it took him 2 hours to prepare the daily required amount. Hyeonse felt he might die of muscle ache in his arms because it was such a laborious process. But as time passed by, he learned to accept it as a learning process. It became a time for meditation and deep thought instead of painful labor.

'I wonder how my family in Gyeongju is doing. How is Daehee my helpful buddy doing? When will I ever become a full-fledged comic book artist? Come to think of it, preparing the ink by **grinding**" the ink stick makes me feel a bit like a **swordsman**" sharpening his **blade**" for battle.'

Working life offered many challenges.

- **grind** [graind] ⓝ,ⓥ reduce to small pieces or particles by pounding or abrading
- **swordsman** [sɔ:rdzmən] ⓝ someone skilled at fencing
- **blade** [bleid] ⓝ a cutting or thrusting weapon

The tiny studio was overcrowded with students and artists. Naturally they had to adhere to strict rules and **hierarchy**▪. As the newest recruit, Hyeonse was the busiest, tending to the needs of all his seniors. That included hand-washing underwears. Hyeonse was grateful to one particular senior artist who didn't change underwear for weeks because that spells less work for Hyeonse. But then there was a down side to that habit. He would infect everyone with ticks. The blood sucking **parasite**▪ thrives under unsanitary conditions. They breed rapidly and victims suffer from itchiness. Thanks to that senior artist, everyone got to experience that sensation.

▪ **hierarchy** [háiərɑ̀ːrki] ⑩ the organization of people at different ranks in an administrative body
▪ **parasite** [pǽrəsàit] ⑩ an animal or plant that lives in or on a host

"What is that stench?"

"Ouch! Something bit me."

"Ticks! Where did they come from?"

And then there was one senior who kept sending Hyeonse on errands late at night. Back in the 1980s, the Korean Government **enforced**[■] a curfew law, preventing people from **loitering**[■] outdoors too late at night. Hyeonse hated this senior who kept sending him out to buy some liquor late at night. But as an obedient and devoted member, he had to do it.

'He does this to me every night! I better be

■ **enforce** [infɔ́ːrs] Ⓥ ensure observance of laws and rules

■ **loiter** [lɔ́itər] Ⓥ hang around, footle

quick and stealthy. Don't want to get caught by the curfew police.'

Unfortunately most shops were closed at such a late hour. Hyeonse had to resort to knocking on closed doors.

"Hello! Please open up."

The owner of the shop got up and opened the door. But she had no kind words for the unwelcomed customer.

"What are you doing here at this hour? Don't

you know you could get arrested? Hurry back home! No sale at this hour!"

"Please, its for my senior artist in our studio. Just one kettle full of makgeolli. If I can't bring it back, he'll kill me."

"You poor thing. Alright then."

"Thank you. But I'm afraid you'll have to put this on our tab as well. I don't have any money with me now."

"What? You can't do that. And this isn't your first time doing that. Don't ever come back to my shop!"

"I'm begging you, please. I will pay you back."

"Oh, alright. Be careful on your way back."

Hyeonse really despised this particular senior artist who keep sending him on this dangerous and difficult errand.

"Welcome back Hyeonse."

"Here's your makgeolli."

"Sit down. We have a test for you."

"What kind of test?"

In the all-male studio, boys will be boys. They wanted to test who is more **gutsy**■. One such test involved running out to a nearby **cemetery**■ during curfew hours. The mission was to plant a flag there and rush back. These were hard times,

---

■ **gutsy** [gʌ́tsi] ⓐ marked by courage and determination in the face of difficulties or danger

■ **cemetery** [sémətèri] ⓝ a tract of land used for burials

but the boys knew how to have fun.

Comic books were becoming a bigger part of Hyeonse's life as time passed by. Painting and erasing over and over again everyday could be a grind for some, but Hyeonse would happily endure any hardship if it meant becoming a comic book artist. Unfortunately while working as a student and an assistant, there was little time to work on his own projects. So he decided to practice making his own comics at night. He would rather sleep less and practice more. But at a small place, **cramped** ▪ up by bodies lying side by side to sleep, he couldn't simply turn on the light at night. So he used a small lamp, covered himself up with blankets and

▪ **cramp** [kræmp] ⓝ.ⓥ suffer from sudden painful contraction of a muscle

painted in that tiny space.

One time, Hyeonse fell asleep without turning off the **lantern**▪, and it overheated, lighting up the blanket along the way. This incident almost led to Hyeonse's **expulsion**▪.

No matter what stood in the way, he lived only to create comic books and learned to get better at it. Whether it was a teacher focused on painting feminine or comical pieces, he was able to learn something from them. And these early lessons helped broaden Hyeonse's range and versatility as an artist.

▪ **lantern** [lǽntərn] ⓝ light in a transparent protective case
▪ **expulsion** [ikspʌ́lʃən] ⓝ the act of forcing out someone or something

5. Taking Flight

Several years passed, Hyeonse returned to his family in his hometown to declare that he will work as a comic book artist. His grandmother strongly opposed this idea, but she could not bend his will.

"Grandma, I can't give up this dream. I will become a comic book artist."

"No. No way. You're supposed to carry on the family name and I can't have you working in such a dishonorable field."

"Trust me, I know this is my calling in life. It is the only thing that makes me happy. I know I will succeed. Grandma, next time we meet, I would have become a famous and respected comic book artist. I promise."

After making this promise to his grandmother, Hyeonse returned to Seoul. He moved to a different studio under the tutelage of a better known artist. Hyeonse quickly gained the respect of his peers as he was great at his job, and got things done quickly. One quick glance at any object or **scenery**[■] was all he needed to remember and then **duplicate**[■] them on paper. His friends began calling him 'The Camera'.

"How do you do it? Your paintings look so vivid. They are comparable to photographs."

"It's nothing. I still have a long way to go. I have to keep pushing myself."

"You are good! You are like a machine! A living, breathing camera. That's what we should call you!"

Hyeonse began working for a teen magazine

■ **scenery** [síːnəri] ⓝ the appearance of a place
■ **duplicate** [djúːplikət] ⓐ,ⓝ,ⓥ make or be an exact copy or copies of something

named ⟨Saesonyeon⟩. Back then, most magazines hired artists to copy popular Japanese comic books. The magazines didn't purchase the rights to these products, but they had Korean artists copying them and published the works anyway. Such was the **prevalent**▪ trend during those times. Young artists like Hyeonse had little power to argue against such flawed systems, so they had to play along.

During those days, comic book artists had little to rely on except their imagination. Unlike today, when any image is accessible through the internet, the artists had to actually go to a zoo to take a look at the animals they have to sketch. So every weekend, Hyeonse would pack some food

▪ **prevalent** [prévələnt] ⓐ most frequent or common

and visit the zoo, and spend all day sketching the animals. During weekdays, he would often skip meals and stay up all night sketching.

Hyeonse got a chance to read various foreign comic books as most magazines he worked for sent him copies of such works. Through this experience, he became certain that comic books can be used as an expressive art form.

Hyeonse at age 25 decided he must create his original work. In 1978, he made his professional debut through a sci-fi comic book titled 『Butterfly Girl and the Underwater World』. He could not contain his excitement after receiving the first copy of his very own comic book.

'The rugged surface of the pages, the fresh ink and my name on the cover. I will remember this moment forever.'

The first order of business after his debut was to **retrieve**■ the original copies of all his previous works from the companies he worked for.

"Chief, how have you been? I'm afraid I need the original copies of my work back."

"Long time no see. What do you need them for?"

"For personal reasons, I need to refer to them to learn and grow further. Please help me out."

■ **retrieve** [ritríːv] ⓥ get or find back

"I see. Let me look into it. It shouldn't take long. You're all grown up. And yet you yearn to improve and mature further as an artist. Fascinating fellow!"

After retrieving these copies, he burned them all. They amounted to some 10 thousand pages.

He felt that these works, created without any of his creative input, had no soul. As he watched them all burn, it fueled his determination to become a true comic book artist.

6. Kachi is Born

The sun was slowly rising. While looking out the window, Hyeonse spoked to himself.

'The sun is already up. It's time to get some shut-eye. I feel like I'm utilizing half a day longer than most people.'

Working until 6am and going to bed only then

was becoming routine for Hyeonse. He wanted to spend more time awake and working than sleeping.

One day, he realized that he needed to create his very own original character if he wants to succeed in this field. Although he was talented at formulating stories and sketching, he was still unable to find that one true character that he could identify with. After working under many different teachers, he learned early on how important and difficult it is to find one's own style. But no matter how long and hard he devoted his time to creating his own character with his own style, he couldn't come up with that one original character.

'My mind's a blank. All of my peers have already developed their own characters and styles, but why can't I? Am I sorely lacking creativity?'

Then, one day, it hit him.

'Is there such a thing as true original pieces? Come to think of it, most comic book characters aren't too different from each other! Why did I assume they were all so different and unique? The key differences were... their attitude and habits! It's the way they are and how they came to be that makes them original and new! It's so simple! Now I know!'

But knowing was only half the battle. He worked on it all day long, yet he would hit a wall.

He turned to his old friend, comic book artist Lee Heejae.

"How do I create my own character?"

"Well, it's easier said than done. Creating something original is no easy task."

The two were having this conversation while relieving themselves at a public bathroom. Heejae **sighed**, and then continued talking.

"Hyeonse, ever noticed how we talk about the

■ **sigh** [sai] ⓝ,ⓥ breathe deeply and heavily

grinds of everyday life even while in the toilet, but most comic book characters are always so deep in thought or seriously discussing topics that seem **farfetched**▪ from our reality?"

Heejae's comment gave Hyeonse an idea. Hyeonse realized that the answer was right under his nose. He concluded that the character should be based on Hyeonse's own trials and **tribulations**▪ in life. From that new starting point, Hyeonse built new and more realistic characters. The fruit of his labor was 'Oh Hyeseong', also known as 'Kachi' a character that became an important part of Korean comic book history.

▪ **farfetched** [fɑːrfetʃed] ⓐ highly imaginative but unlikely

▪ **tribulation** [tribjuléiʃən] ⓝ an annoying or frustrating or catastrophic event

'I'll use all of my real life experiences and memories to breathe life into Kachi. An **introverted**▪ loner with a tragic childhood, who has a strong sense of justice, and doesn't **succumb**▪ to evil temptations! Kachi will be like no other character before him.'

Just as he expected, 'Kachi' or 'Oh Hyeseong' took shape as a stand out character. He was a tragic outsider, very different from the wholesome and cheerful heroic characters of past. He is a man who gives everything to shield the woman he loves from his tragic past and the dark future ahead. But now the challenging task was coming up with

▪ **introverted** [íntrəvə̀:rtid] ⓐ given to examining own sensory and perceptual experiences
▪ **succumb** [səkʌm] ⓥ consent reluctantly, be fatally overwhelmed

the right look. Hyeonse was confident of creating various characters appropriate for different genres. And he wanted his character to be a chameleon that would change from comical to serious in seconds. Hyeonse decided to try something that's never been done before. Back in those days, most comic book characters stuck with one fixed genre throughout. But Hyeonse's Oh Hyeseong would change into a romantic character when around his girl 'Eomji', and then into a comical one around his buddies, and again, put on the face of a deadly charismatic action star when facing his arch rival 'Ma Dongtak'. In order to help readers understand that the character that looks so

▲ Lee Hyeonse, 『The Baseball Team』, 1982

different at different times was the one and same, Hyeonse came up with a unique hairstyle for 'Oh Hyeseong'. He would **stub**∎ his brush several times to form the 'Kachi hairstyle'. Anyone could tell it was 'Oh Hyeseong' no matter how different his face looked, thanks to his unique hairstyle. This original character would go on to star in many of Hyeonse's hits, including 『The Baseball Team』, 『The Raven of the Border』, 『Ring of Hell』, and 『Nambeol War Stories』.

∎ **stub** [stʌb] ⓝ.ⓥ extinguish by crushing

7. Censored, Time and Again

During the 1970s and the 80s, the Korean Government imposed strict **censorship**■ over cultural or artistic materials. Censorship was especially strict on comic books, beginning from the late 1960s. Artists were not allowed to show scenes that depict poverty or extreme sorrow. Their reason: Such scenes could instil anti-social sentiment within readers. Such extreme censorship

---

■ **censorship** [sénsərʃip] ⓝ counterintelligence achieved by banning or deleting any information of value to the enemy

frustrated comic book artists of those years. With such restrictions, it was difficult to have a natural flow to their stories. Changing the scenes over and over again due to the demands of censorship boards became the **norm**[■]. Making so many changes ultimately led to books that had flawed continuity or story lines that don't make much sense.

"This is so frustrating!"

"I know! Why do they keep picking on the smallest details?"

"I had to cut out chunks of important bits."

"This is why comic books can't get better!"

■ **norm** [nɔːrm] ⓝ a standard or model or pattern regarded as typical

Many artists were frustrated with heavy censorship. It was especially harder for Hyeonse who tried to create realistic stories using realistic characters. Most of his characters were **lonesome**[■], **rebellious**[■] outcasts. Naturally the censorship board members were not pleased. Hyeonse has dedicated his career to improving the comic book industry and he wasn't about to let censorship stand in his way. He would change the **backdrop**[■] to a foreign country or delete scenes as requested by the censorship board, and then drew it back on afterwards. He will always find a way to fight censorship. His 1982 piece titled 『The Raven of the Border』 was under fire by the censorship board.

■ **lonesome** [lóunsəm] ⓐ marked by dejection from being alone

■ **rebellious** [ribéljəs] ⓐ resisting control or authority

■ **backdrop** [bǽkdràp] ⓝ scenery hung at back of stage

"The scenes where the hero executes his **vengeance**▪ plan are too violent. Get rid of all these scenes."

"Okay…"

Hyeonse would simply reply he would do as ordered. When showing his final product, he would **conceal**▪ the scenes ordered to be deleted with a blank piece of paper. Upon gaining the authority's approval, Hyeonse would remove the paper and include such scenes back in his final product. Many of those scenes were **pivotal**▪ in moving the story along, so he couldn't give them up. He was ordered to make the faces of the characters in 『The

▪ **vengeance** [véndʒəns] ⓝ the act of taking revenge
▪ **conceal** [kənsíːl] ⓥ prevent from being seen or discovered
▪ **pivotal** [pívətl] ⓐ being of crucial importance

Baseball Team」 less shady. Hoping that his readers will notice his original design for the characters, Hyeonse would **dab**▪ off some of the darkness ever so slightly. The artists of that era had to constantly find new ways to protect their creations from being **butchered**▪ by censorship. It may sound farfetched today, but many publishing companies were shut down and artists were sent to jail by order of censorship committees back in those days.

▪ **dab** [dæb] ⓝ,ⓥ touch or hit lightly

▪ **butcher** [bútʃər] ⓝ,ⓥ ruin or make a botch of something

8. 『The Baseball Team』 Syndrome

『The Baseball Team』, published in 1982, is arguably the most revolutionary comic book in Korean history. In 1981 when professional baseball was launched in Korea, it was a golden era for Korean pro baseball. Hyeonse was trying to come up with the storyline for his next piece. Writer Kim Mingi's 『The Baseball Team』 captivated Hyeonse instantly. Most comic books back in those days were mostly less than 3 volumes. Naturally Kim Mingi wrote barely enough for 3 books.

"This is amazing! It's going to be an instant bestseller. Could you write more? I think the story can go on for much longer!"

"Ha ha ha! What a coincidence, I actually thought up of enough stories to last 30 volumes."

30 volumes for a comic book series was unheard of back then. Comic book artists were discouraged from creating books longer than 400 pages all together, due to various censorship rules. Thanks to the explosive popularity of pro baseball,

『The Baseball Team』 received incredible response upon publication. Comic book stores and comic book cafes were packed with customers.

And the star of Hyeonse's latest work, 'Kachi', became loved nationwide. It's common to see trend-conscious people imitating new hair styles of popular idols. Similarly Kachi's hair style became a hit. Many comic book artists imitated the hair style, attitude and the lines of the popular character. Too many comic book stores and cafes began using that name.

"I thought I just passed 'Kachi comic book café'."

▲ Lee Hyeonse, 『The Baseball Team』, 1982

"I think we did. Wait! There's another one over there!"

"How many 'Kachi comic book cafes' are there in this neighborhood?"

With his character names like 'Kachi', 'Eomji' and 'Ma Dongtak' being used everywhere without his consent, Hyeonse registered for the exclusive rights to these names. 『The Baseball Team』 was more than just a successful, well-made comic book. It helped alter perceptions about comic books.

That it's not just for children and unsuitable for grown-ups. The detailed and complex story and character relations appealed to both young and old.

There is a popular incident that proves this point. An avid reader of 『The Baseball Team』 got caught reading it in class and had his copy confiscated. But the teacher, who grew curious began reading it. He ended up staying all night, immersed in the story. The following day, with blood-shot eyes, the teacher asked that student.

"When is the next volume coming up?"

Hyeonse is hailed as an artist that changed comic books from simply being dubbed 'childish objects' to an independent art form that can be appreciated by all. The explosive success and popularity of 『The Baseball Team』 led various media outlets to focus on the work and even hold thorough discussions and debates over the book. 『The Baseball Team』 is easily named as the first Korean comic book to be enjoyed by fans of all gender and age groups, while firmly placing comic books to the **mainstream** of popular culture.

Thanks to 『The Baseball Team』, Lee Hyeonse was able to become a famous artist. Being one of the more handsome comic book artist among peers certainly helped improve his popularity as well. Thanks to his success and good looks, he was

---

■ **mainstream** [méinstriːm] ⑩ the prevailing current of thought

offered to star in a TV beer commercial. Filming began at 3am and finished late at night. It was a 3-part series. The final part was filmed in a park in Monument Valley, USA. While filming Hyeonse was greeted warmly by devoted fans of his work, including the many commercials he starred in.

『The Baseball Team』 was even made into a movie. Jeon Yeongrok, one of the hottest singers of the 1980s was a big fan of the comic book, and he recommended the book to film director Lee Jangho. Lee Jangho, considered to be unreachable as he is in high demand everywhere, actually called Hyeonse up to talk about a movie idea.

"Is this Mr. Lee Hyeonse?"

"Speaking."

"I'm director Lee Jangho. I wanted to talk to you about turning 『The Baseball Team』 into a movie."

"My comic book... into a movie?"

Hyeonse jumped with joy at the proposal. No original Korean comic book has ever been made into a movie before. Production went on smoothly and the movie opened in 1986. 〈Lee Jangho's Baseball Team〉 was successful, drawing 400 thousand audience nationwide. "Whatever it takes to make you happy" a romantic line **quoted**▪

▪ **quote** [kwout] ⓝ.ⓥ repeat a passage from

by 'Oh Hyeseong', the lead character inspired musicians to write and compose a song titled ⟨From Me to You⟩. It was included in the movie's original sound track, and became a chart-topper.

9. Turning Point

『The Baseball Team』 marked the turning point in Hyeonse's career. 'Oh Hyeseong' evolved into a more complete and detailed character after this series was completed. Hyeonse became so popular that 8 different companies wanted to publish monthly issues of his new works. Although Hyeonse loved his job and he continued to create amazing stories and characters, he apparently overexerted himself. Fatigue took over, Hyeonse was rushed to the hospital in 1986. He got hepatitis. Even while he was recovering, he yearned to get back to work. He spent his bed-ridden days thinking about ideas for new stories.

'I need to elevate comic books to a new level. It shouldn't be a mere disposable entertainment medium. I want to create an informative piece that is moving. Something that feels different everytime it is read.'

Seoul was busy preparing to host the 1988 Olympic Games. A lot of low-income laborers

worked in an industrial complex in Guro-dong.
That the working environment was very poor.
Around 60 thousand workers lived together in
tiny rooms without bathrooms. The rooms were
clustered together, and it looked like a beehive.
Hyeonse was shocked to learn about the tragic and
difficult lives of the workers in this 'Beehive Town'.

'They live such difficult lives, and have no one
to listen to their tragic stories. The world doesn't
care about their pain and hardship. Their stories
must be heard.'

And that is how Hyeonse began work on 『The

Report of the Daughter-in-law's Rice Flower⌋.

But because it was so different from the action-packed sports comics he created before, it caught the readers by surprise. Some even had a hard time believing it was Hyeonse's work. But through this project, Hyeonse was able to elevate himself to a new level as an artist. He continued to work hard to collaborate with other artists to prove that comic books are more than just a simple source of entertainment.

Hyeonse was eager to turn any idea, regardless of genre, into a comic book. He was planning on creating a science fiction or sci-fi comic book. After creating works that dealt with issues and stories related with the people around him, he felt it was time to go back to his roots. Hyeonse, being a nature lover, thought about the possible future of mankind.

'Everything has a beginning and an end. The rain, the wind, the sun, the clouds, the salmon that fight their way upstream, and the majestic eagle that soars high above are all amazing. But what about mankind? In the name of progress, they destroy the ecosystem. Perhaps humans are a plague the earth can do without. If there is one thing that makes mankind unique and perhaps of some value is the fact that we are capable of love.'

That is how 『Armageddon』, a story about the last space war came to be. Hyeonse immediately began working with a writer on an epic sci-fi tale that takes place in space. Back then, the only Korean SF comic books were typical, small-scale super-robot stories. What Hyeonse was planning was beyond what any Korean comic book artist dreamed of. But as exciting as this project was, realizing such a goal proved to be very challenging. Korea back then, sorely lacked **inspirational**[■] sources for Hyeonse to base his sci-fi related materials on. He needed to see more images that would inspire him to paint the future world to be depicted in his new comic book, but he had no

■ **inspirational** [inspəréiʃənl] ⓐ imparting a divine influence on the mind and soul

where to turn to. Hyeonse could rely only on his imagination. He even built scaled models for the space ships to be featured in his book. As a result, when 『Armageddon』was released, once again Hyeonse marked another turning point in Korean comic book history. The readers loved it. And the publishers wanted Hyeonse to produce more issues fast.

"Hyeonse! The readers' response is amazing! We need more, fast. Can you produce 50 pages per week?"

"That would require the help of all the assistants your company can provide me."

50 pages for one comic book series featured in a monthly magazine was an incredible amount. Hyeonse had to put everything on hold and focus on 『Armageddon』 only.

10. First Grave Error

Film makers would not leave Hyeonse alone because of 『Armageddon』. Numerous production companies asked for the rights to produce it into a movie. But Hyeonse waited patiently for the right partner.

"How about making it into a movie?"

"I'm afraid the director and actors you chose

are not right for the project. It's not happening."

Time passed by and there was no 『Armageddon』 the movie yet. But in the mid-1990s, one production company suggested creating an animated TV series of 『Armageddon』.
A special committee dedicated to the Armageddon project was formed, and various companies began investing in the production.

"We have numerous companies eager to invest in the Armageddon animation project!"
"Such a phenomenon is unprecedented."
"We have more than 4-point-4 million dollars

invested so far. ⟨Armageddon⟩ is going to be big."

"I'm grateful to our investors, but more importantly I'm proud to be a part of such a bold animation project. Let's do a great job."

"Let's do that!"

Back then, it was rare for numerous companies to eagerly invest in a single production. And the sum that amounted to was unheard of in the animation realm. Using domestic talent, technology and funds to create a grand scale animated film was a thrilling challenge for Hyeonse and the production crew. Fans of Hyeonse were **brimming**▪ with anticipation. And Hyeonse was

▪ **brimming** [brímin] ⓐ filled to capacity

excited about the prospects of this revolutionary project. Initially started out as a TV series, the Armageddon team decided to turn it into a full length feature film instead. Hyeonse took on the task of directing the entire project.

"Mr. Lee, we would love to have you do the storyboard for ⟨Armageddon⟩."

"I've never worked on animated films before, I don't know if I'm right for the job."

"Who better for the job than you? It is your story after all."

A storyboard is like strips of sketches designed

to help the crew better understand how the story flows in the movie. The Korean animation industry was at its infancy back then, and Hyeonse didn't fully understand exactly how different directing animated film is to creating comic books. Hyeonse already had his hands full with his new comic book titled 『Nambeol War Stories』. He had to work on 『Nambeol War Stories』 first to meet the monthly deadlines. Naturally work on 〈Armageddon〉 storyboard was delayed continuously. Making things worse, Hyeonse got little outside help, as Korea sorely lacked animated film experts. Even the sound effects for the project, which was tasked to a studio in the US wasn't going smoothly.

Although the project had a most promising start, it wasn't progressing smoothly. All the complications **snowballed** ▪ into an unsuccessful final product. ⟨Armageddon⟩ opened in 1996 and was a box office disaster. For the first time in his career, Hyeonse tasted bitter failure. Regardless, ⟨Armageddon⟩ was the first grand-scale animated film attempt in Korea. And to ensure his failure can serve as a reliable case-study for next generation film makers, Hyeonse even worked with his production crew on documenting the reasons behind ⟨Armageddon⟩'s failure.

In 1997, shortly after the painful experience, Hyeonse had to brace himself for another deep

---

▪ **snowball** [snoubɔːl] ⓝ,ⓥ increase or accumulate at a rapidly accelerating rate

impact. His 100-volume comic book series titled 『Mythology of the Heavens』 was on the **verge** ▪ of being banned in Korea. This was a big blow to Hyeonse, as he was dedicated to this project back in the 1980s when he was working on 『The Baseball Team』.

'In European nations and even in China, they have their own mythology that details the beginning of mankind. Korea has her own, but it stops short after the very beginning chapter.'

Hyeonse began his research on such mythologies of various countries. It took him

▪ **verge** [vəːrdʒ] ⓝ,ⓥ a region marking a boundary

decades of research and planning, and finally he published the book. But his dreams were **shattered**▪ by the walls of reality. The publishers signed a contract to release 100 volumes, and this incident happened after the 6th volume was published. His work was classified as harmful and unethical. Hyeonse went to battle in the court of law for 6 years to **defend**▪ his artistic rights.

▪ **shatter** [ʃǽtər] ⓥ break into many pieces, damage or destroy

▪ **defend** [difénd] ⓥ protect against a challenge or attack

11. 『Mythology of the Heavens』 Stirs Controversy

The battle surrounding 『Mythology of the Heavens』 pitted the comic book artists against the Prosecutor's Office. Korean society began to have a more positive perception of comic books, thanks to efforts of Hyeonse and many more devoted artists. But there were people in power who perceived comic books as harmful materials.

"Lee Hyeonse will pay a fine of 2700 dollars."

Hyeonse had to pay the **hefty** **fine**. He felt it wasn't fair. Professionals in the comic book industry formed an alliance around Hyeonse. As the **prosecutors** continued to have their way with comic books, some quit, while others held protests. It was very rare to see artists, who are so individualistic gather together for a unified cause. Unfortunately, as a result of the incident, Korea's comic book market shrank in size greatly.

Hyeonse was engaged in that legal battle for over 6 years. And he grew weary and confused. He wondered if his work might actually be harmful to readers, and became frustrated with the oppressive police and prosecutors. Making matters worse, his aunt and grandmother passed away.

Losing two of the people he loved the most dealt Hyeonse a tremendous blow. They helped him through thick and thin, even when he had a difficult time coming to grasp with the family secret. The timing could not be worse. Hyeonse was already feeling completely drained, after the 6-year court battle. Thankfully, his colleagues were there to support him and rally him on.

"Don't give up Hyeonse! We are right behind you! Every comic book artist will join forces to

help you win this battle for your artistic rights!"

"No! I won't ever give up. I have done nothing wrong and I will not pay a single penny as penalty for my art work. I will keep fighting and I will win. I will not give up."

On June 2002, Hyeonse was finally freed of all charges. Thanks to his efforts, comic books became accepted as an art form more widely in the nation, and the Government could no longer easily pick on comic book artists for their creative expressions.

For Hyeonse's unyielding efforts to defend the comic book industry, the Ministry of Culture,

Sports and Tourism named him Artist of the Year for 2005. It was the first time a comic book artist was awarded this honor.

12. New Challenges

Korean National Police Agency's mascot is 'Podori'. This character helped Korean police grow closer to the people with its friendly image. He is vigilantly on the lookout for crime with his wide eyes, listens to the needs and wants of the citizens with his huge ears, welcome people with his million-dollar smile, track down the suspect using his acute sense of smell and fully utilizes his sense of justice and fairness in any situation. Lee Hyeonse is the genius behind this creation.

'The 『Mythology of the Heavens』 incident' did dampen his passion for comic books, but that didn't last long. Hyeonse got back on his feet and continued to create more works. His biggest asset was positive thinking. It was thanks to this quality, Hyeonse was able to get over any discouraging experiences and rekindle his love for comic books.

'We are all fearful of failing. But one failure doesn't spell the end of the world. No need to fear, I'll just keep at it, and continue to create my own path in life.'

Hyeonse continued to publish new works. In 1997, he was hired as a professor at the Sejong University department of animation. Hyeonse gladly accepted the role, knowing that he can help aspiring artists learn necessary skills to jump into the field. Students and parents continued to come to Hyeonse with questions.

"What is your secret? How do you continue to create new and exciting comic books without taking long breaks?"

"To be a good comic book artist, you need to do two things. First, you must learn to absorb new things and also to get them out of your system.

Read, listen to music and watch movies. And make it a habit to write journals. Write short and concise paragraphs. That way you'll learn to express more with less. Secondly, always carry a sketch pad and draw whatever you see. The more you do this, the better you'll get at sketching things quickly. It is important to be able to sketch fast, so you can capture the essence of what needs to be drawn quickly. There is no secret or shortcuts to becoming a good comic book artist. To be doing this for life, you need to have your own philosophy and keep at it."

In 2002, Hyeonse established 'Lee Hyeonse

Entertainment'. The company supported various comic book and animation projects. He was also named the 23rd chair of the Korea Cartoonists Association, and was named an honorary police inspector on the 56th Police Day for his contributions to the force. Not only that, Hyeonse also served as a member of the Korea Publication Ethics Commission. Thanks to his efforts to raise awareness of the Dokdo issue, he was also named an honorary captain of the Dokdo Guards. No matter how many different titles he is given, Hyeonse would only introduce himself as a comic book artist. His only reason for undertaking all these different tasks and roles was to broaden his horizon to grow as an artist and a teacher.

For quite some time in Korea, any survey on favorite comic book characters would have the name 'Kachi' and 'Eomji' topping the list. But as time passed by, a new generation of comic book artists and readers surfaced.

'There's a new generation of readers today... So this is where I stand now.'

Hyeonse's lifelong dream was to create comic books that anyone can enjoy, regardless of age or gender. It suddenly occurred to him that most of his avid readers have now grown up. That is why Hyeonse decided to work on educational comic books for children. He felt that history is an important subject that should better appeal to young readers. And so in 2005, Hyeonse began work on comic books designed to help readers better understand Korean history. He did all this while working on his original works as well.

13. Comic Book Artist Through and Through

Hyeonse, the man who grew up with nothing but comic books on his mind, had one **immutable** ▪ principle: Never create sequels. Even when huge offers were made to Hyeonse to create a sequel to 『The Baseball Team』, he rejected them all. His fans would be glowing with anticipation for Hyeonse's next piece, and every time, he would respond in kind with something incredible and

▪ **immutable** [imjúːtəbl] ⓐ not subject or susceptible to change or variation in form or quality or nature

original. Hyeonse spoke about how he wants to spend his twilight years.

"I decided long ago that I want to become a grandfather devoted to creating fairy tales for the little ones. If I'm given the opportunity to continue doing what I do in my 70s and I am still able, I'd be able to create works that are distinctly different from the products of younger artists."

In one of his columns, he described he summed up his one true love in life.

"I just need to draw one more page of pictures

before going to bed. Completing that one piece of work before the sun sets everyday will eventually lead to an improved version of myself as an artist. It's not about reaching new heights, but about becoming as good as I can be."

Life was difficult for Lee Hyeonse while growing up. Despite poverty and a tragic family history, Hyeonse could dream of greatness thanks to comic books. His journey was anything but smooth sailing. But, fuelled by his passion for the craft and devotion to his readers, Hyeonse was able to overcome all **odds**[■]. He is one of the most respected comic book artists of Korea. It

■ **odds** [adz] ⓝ distress or suffering

was his lifelong dream to become and live as a comic book artist. And now he is living the dream. Lee Hyeonse is a comic book artist through and through, now and forever.

영어로 읽는 세계 속 한국인 ❺

LEE HYEONSE 이현세

초판 1쇄 인쇄 2013년 01월 22일
초판 1쇄 발행 2013년 01월 28일

지은이	Daniel Choy(최진완), Yun Hyeji(윤혜지)
펴낸이	이준경
편집	박윤선
디자인	김인엽
마케팅	오정옥
펴낸곳	㈜영진미디어
출판 등록	2011년 1월 7일 제141-81-22416
주소	경기도 파주시 문발동 파주출판도시 504-3 ㈜영진미디어
전화	031-955-4955
팩스	031-955-4959
이메일	book@yjmedia.net
홈페이지	www.yjbooks.com
이미지	이현세 화실 제공(65, 76쪽)
종이	㈜월드페이퍼
인쇄	㈜현문자현
녹음	㈜미디어뱅크포유
음악감독	김형석

값 12,000원
ISBN 978-89-969425-7-3